Rebecca Hood

Tarot

For Beginners

A Complete Guide to Discover the Secrets of
Tarot Reading

THE FOOL.

THE MAGICIAN.

THE LOVERS.

THE SUN .

Table of Contents

What is Tarot?

The Tarot (also known as Tarock, Tarokk, Tarot, and similar names) is a family of trick-taking card games. The game has expanded to 78 cards, which contain legal documents for each of the four semi-regular dress, to win a permanent 21 cards, and a kind of "wild card" with the name "mad" or "I'm sorry." Even Though it is regarded primarily by many as a means of predicting the future or divination, the Tarot deck was created in Northern Italy during the 15th century as play cards. The idea of winning a suit that survives in such popular card games as spades and Hearts comes from the Tarot game.

The myth of the Egyptian origin of tarot cards, although once common, has long been revealed by later scholars, before the eighteenth. For centuries, there is no trace of tarot cards used for occultism or prophecy. Popular tarot readings at Renaissance fairs are a creative license taken with a historical fact and should not be considered authentic. Contrary to popular belief, classic playing cards were not derived from Tarot card games, and the Fool is not related to The Joker of classic playing cards. The Joker was created in the United States during the 19th century originally for the card game Euchre.

There are two types of Tarot deck.

The appropriate Italian Tarot

The traditional game of Italian, suitable for coins, cups, swords, and batons, is currently favored by those who use Tarot cards, divination. However, in some countries such as Italy and Switzerland, these decks are still used for the game. Those who practice tarot prophecy often call coins "pentagons" and "wands." With a few exceptions, trump the Italian Tarot adapted the scene varies little from one platform to another and are often regarded by Tarot readers as containing a symbolic meaning. The depiction of Papessa (II) and the pope (in) on related Italian Tarot Cards has been controversial in some regions. In Switzerland, these images were replaced by images of Juno (II) and Jupiter (V.). In Bologna, the papal figurines with Empress (III) and Emperor (IV) were replaced by four figures of moresche, which are not numbered and serve as triumphs of the same status in the Bologna Tarot variety. The system of Italian or Spanish costumes is not limited to tarot cards. This suit system is a common regional model of classic playing cards in southern Europe and Latin America.

French tarot

Tip card with a French or international outfit, tiles, heart, spades, Clover is now used in countries such as France and Austria for the game. In France and southern Germany, Roman numerals have been abandoned in favor of Arabic numerals, while in some countries, such as Austria, Roman numerals are still used. Trump Images appropriate to the French Tarot often depict scenes of people at work and play, and real and mythological animals and landscapes, the regional space. In some regions such as Austria and southern Germany, the game is reduced to 54 cards with the removal of the lower pip card. Unlike the relevant Italian decks, there is a wide variety of images on French tarot cards. On the decks of the French Tarot, a mad man is often depicted as a musician, harlequin, or other types of artist. French Tarot Cards are rarely used for divination.

Common rules of the game

At each turn, players must follow, if possible. If the seeds are not possible, it will be necessary to reproduce the resource. If the players are empty in the suit played and are also empty in the cards, then any card can be played. The winner of one round leads another.

There is a noticeable variation in how a fool or an excuse is used. In countries like France and Italy, The Fool is a "wild card" that can be played in any order, to avoid having to follow suit, while in some countries like Austria and South Germany, the Fool is simply the biggest asset.

Many modern tarot games include offers to determine who will become the recipient and play alone against other players. In some tarot cards with four or more players, the recipient of the card called the king or the high-ranking card chooses a partner, whose identity remains secret until the called card is played.

The values of Cards where "n" is often equal to 1, 2, 3 or 4 depending on the type of game played, are presented as follows:

Trump XXI (21), Trump I (1), the excuse or the fool, and the four Kings are worth $4 + 1 / n$ each

The four queens are worth $3 + 1 / n$ each

The four Knights or Knights are worth $2 + 1 / n$ each

The four sockets are worth $1 + 1 / n$ each

All other cards have a value of $1 / n$ each

The usual goal of Tarot card games is to score more card points, as well as any other bonus point, which may also be available depending on the regional variant you are playing.

Tarot reading and divination

Although they were originally designed for card games, Tarot Cards are generally regarded by many as a splitting tool, especially in regions where Tarot card games remain largely unknown. There are many published bridges that are dedicated today for the purpose of divination. The most famous bridge designed for divination or "getting information" is the Tarot Rider Waite Smith.

Using fortune-telling cards, they are arranged in a pattern. These patterns, usually in the form of a cross, are known as "throws" or "spreads." "Queerer," which is the one who aspires to read the tarot cards, mixes the package and asks the question in the cards. The question could be "yes" or "no" of a more general type or nature. The reader organizes the cards into the proliferation of choice and allegedly tries to answer the question using the cards as a guide. The divinatory interpretation of a Tarot card often depends on the vertical or inverted direction of the card or its juxtaposition with other cards. Sometimes only 22 cards from the Tarot deck are used. These cards, called "Major Arcane" by Tarot readers, include 21 triumphs and one Fool. The remaining 56 cards are called "minor arcane."

Not all Tarot readers call themselves "fortune tellers" when they claim not to use cards for predictive purposes. In recent years, "psychological" rather than paranormal interpretations have been guided by a context in which a lot of tarot data is visible. These tarot data are called "introspective" in nature and do not make supernatural or prophetic statements. Tarot reading has recently become popular in some circles as a reflection tool in an attempt to increase your creativity. It should be noted, however, that there is no empirical evidence of psychic phenomena or therapeutic benefits of Tarot data.

Different Types of Tarot Packs

Initially, tarot cards were the type of game in Italy. However, people adopted them in the psychic reading and turned out to be accurate. Today, it remains one of the most popular psychic tools in the West, and many people believe in the value of this gain. There are many types of tarot cards, and some of them include:

Ator: it has a refreshing new look that makes it suitable for the next generation psychic readings. He uses adorable characters, which is the reason for his popularity among many people.

Benedetti is on a richly painted gold leaf. This is the ideal choice for readers who want to add a touch of class and character to their service. Visconti's maps inspired them.

Cat people tarot: for those who want to glimpse the Earth that is far away, Cat People tarot is a perfect choice. Expresses human imagination with mystics and cats.

Some psychological readers have adopted the psychedelic chromatic approach to their psychological data. For them, the Smith Tarot column is a perfect choice. The most unusual and least used modern tarot is a curious tarot. It is distinguished by strange characters that attract the attention of many people. This is a rare type of Tarot card because readers are afraid that it will frighten customers.

The Golden Tarot: for great thinkers, it is available. Many readers have used gold tarot cards in the past.

International tarot icon: for a more fun approach to tarot data, an international Tarot icon from Switzerland is available. This is their version of traditional tarot data.

Love craft tarot: for fans of Ancient Writings, this tarot is a tribute to one of the ancient writers.

Tarot de Marseille: for the best divination for ordinary people, Tarot de Marseille is easily available and accessible in many stores around the world. It was also common for people to use tarot cards for meditation purposes.

Thin: thin Tarot contains about 97 tarot cards more than any other set of tarot cards. Many consider it one of the most powerful oracle cards. For New Tarot students, the Palladini Tarot deck is best suited. Connect the future with the old Tarot data. It represents elements of ancient Egyptian Art, so it prefers art lovers.

For a new generation of Tarot readers, Phoenix Tarot Cards are more suitable. This is a product of the 20th century. It includes bright colors, and therefore very pleasing to the eye.

Many people go for tarot data to predict the events of his future and the luck or tragedy that may happen. Fear of the unknown is a determining factor for Tarot business data. Depending on their preferences, tarot readers can choose one of the above tarot cards for their business.

How Does Tarot Reading Work?

People often ask how tarot cards, which are collected by the game in random order, can significantly affect the lives of people. It is generally excluded that the tarot cards may not communicate the action you need in a given situation, but rather to give you options, or different directions that you can take. There are many theories about how tarot cards can be so effective. We will examine two of the main theories behind tarot cards in this article.

The first of these theories about the functioning of tarot reading is synchronicity. It is believed that the universe will lead us in the right direction by accident. Basically, these are signs that say, "Hey, do this" or "you should try it." The use of quantum mechanics can partially explain synchronicity and tarot cards. Without going into a full-blown discussion on quantum mechanics, it is safe to say that there are forces in quantum mechanics that have a very real effect on physical objects. It is believed that these energies affect the cards that read tarot cards.

Another Tarot theory is projection. Some believe that we project our beliefs and thoughts about reading tarot and get the result we expect. In other words, you'll find what you're looking for. If this theory of Tarot is true, then the tarot can become a very useful tool. I mean that it will help you connect with your true desires, emotions, and feelings, which are grown in your subconscious mind. Tarot reading, when it comes to research in our subconscious, may be related to the ink point test that we all know. I should say that Tarot Cards are more support to find out what's inside, and a way to talk to your Higher Self.

To perform a tarot reading, you don't need the funds, but some believe that means it is better for the energy they provide. There are two different types of tarot data. The first is the question of the Tarot. It is there that tarot reading is used to answer a particular question. As a rule, you are looking for an answer, "yes or no." Try to look at this kind of tarot reading as a guide to help you make a decision. When you ask a question, try to ask in a general overview, with some details, but not too detailed. When you ask a question in tarot, it is also better to focus the question on you. I am referring to questions about what can be done to change, improve, or change the situation. It is also better to ask the question in a neutral way. Try not to ask the question from a narrow point of view. This will give you a wider range of possible answers and solutions. Of course, when doing a tarot, you want to stay positive in your questions and expectations.

Another type of Tarot is the so-called open reading. This kind of tarot reading is designed to give you a complete overview of your life. When doing this type of tarot reading, you can be a little specific and get information on such areas as Love, Money, Health, and relationships.

When the tarot is made, usually, the person who receives the reading shuffles the cards. It's time to stay in the moment and focus on what you want to discover by reading tarot cards. After the game has been mixed, the person who makes the Tarot Reading will put the cards in a scatter. In a tarot reading, the placement of cards in the span makes sense with the card itself. Different Tarot Cards are used depending on the nature of your question, the reader, and the allotted time.

Surprisingly, tarot cards can be extremely accurate. I strongly recommend people to try to experiment with reading tarot. I think you may be surprised by the answers that come to mind, as well as the problems that are solved.

How Self Development with the Tarot works

You can think about why you want to read tarot cards, and you can focus on the things that help tarot cards reading, what you have in mind. Try asking a question before you see the tarot reader. Do not think that Tarot Cards are designed to match yes or no. If you see the leadership in the Tarot from the reader, you can also feel better at the end of the session. Also, ask reasonable questions. You can also have a clearer view of how to see further into the future.

Some may feel as if Tarot has helped to overcome the situation, which could stand in the presence of life and may eventually see a change. Numbers can be useful in some decisions in your life. They can lead you. Some people need guidance only for a short time when collecting ideas. There are many interpretations of some tarot cards.

Even if you are a beginner, you can still read tarot cards. The best resources you can find on the internet regarding the type of Tarot that you want to use, whether it be online, face to face, or by email, CD or tape, or even books. There are also various articles available for reading in all of the above items that you can refer to. The sites are available for anyone to check out the different and variable Tarot Cards. Tarot cards for centuries claim that they offer or even help to answer all the provocative questions in life.

Tarot cards have advantages and limitations. Everyone decides no matter where he is in his life. Tarot does not work miracles and does not replace any medical care and other medications. Tarot cannot physically help you with any problem that you may have; they can only guide you. They cannot answer whether you will marry or have a child on a given day or date.

There are different sets of cards, depending on the type of Tarot card or packages that you can read. If you are interested in reading tarot cards, you can always search the internet for more questions that you can lay on the cards. Tarot cards can be very accurate in terms of events or what happened to this person. The Internet is the fastest way to find out more information about tarot cards.

Tarot data is available to people if they need to contact them and compare them by images or numbers on tarot cards. People can be emailed Tarot Cards. It is entirely up to the individual if they want to know by different methods. There's an encyclopedia on tarot cards.

You can also do a personal journal once the Tarot is being taught, and maybe a reflection of what a person did in this life is the way of life.

There are also courses that can be taught on tarot cards. There are many websites that can be checked; also, many pictures of tarot cards can be seen on them as well.

There are many decks or tarot cards that can vary around the world; it serves many purposes in your life and journey. Tarot has a confusing history. Cards can always be studied on the course, if possible. The results of tarot cards can be achieved by analyzing the card. Tarot cards can be a good thing when you focus on what you're thinking right now. Good luck reading the Tarot. Bring more tarot messages.

What is Paranormal Tarot Cards Reading?

The history of paranormal Tarot Cards is something that is disguised by time. There are some testimonials and scientists who combine the source of the Tarot with that of ancient Egypt. At the same time, other teachers and the researchers suggest that the spelling of the sources of happiness with a very ancient bohemian refinement. However, more scientists add an Italian source to the tarot cards, and it is believed that Tarot cards have become psychic tools near 1400. From this experience, many different types have evolved and are only used now. One of the popular Bridges is the Rider-Waite Bridge.

A typical tarot deck contains 78 cards consisting of the four seeds seen in normal card games, which are hearts, diamonds, shovels, and clubs. The Latin version of the tarot game has a different set of outfits. These are swords, batons, mugs, and coins. Like a normal game, the tarot cards are numbered from one to ten plus four court cards, jack, queen, king, and Ace.

The difference between the tarot deck and the regular deck is 21 divine cards known as major Arcans. The equivalent tease in the game Tarot is called a fool, or an excuse. A fool can take all four seeds and act as the strongest good.

Reading a tarot card is easy because each trump card has a separate meaning. However, if you want to read the meaning of collecting cards, you need to make an interpretation. These maps have astrological links to data located in the context of the Octavian calendar. It is believed that tarot cards easily describe the physical and emotional characteristics of the subject.

The rich and centuries-old tradition of tarot reading is constantly evolving over time. Methods of interpretation of tarot cards continue to develop to achieve the culture in which they live. Changing the meaning can also contribute to the development of the Charter itself. Elements of the Tarot Card today are very different from what they were before.

Many tarot data are done face to face. You can find someone who reads tarot cards in your area by doing an online search, check local ads, or asking in an occult library. You should come prepared with a question or query much of the time, and you may find that if you can get useful ideas from the reading, it is more of a perceptive tool than a truly esoteric tool. Each Tarot reader has his own preferences on how to arrange cards and read them; however, one can reasonably expect that more complex and longer reading will be more expensive.

You can also have tarot reading on your phone. If you cannot find a local person who makes tarot reading or prefer extra discretion, it may be a good choice. Although you should expect that reading tarot on your phone will be quite expensive, avoid questionable minute-by-minute billing services. There are reliable Tarot readers who provide data over the phone at a reasonable flat rate. Some may also offer online readings for a small amount, and provide their interpretation of the maps through email.

Tarot cards have existed for centuries and have been used in many cultures for divination purposes. There are different card layouts, and there are different card reading methods that card readers use. The interpretation of Tarot Cards is based on the position of the card and the different symbols of each card.

Amateur Tarot Card Readings

As a beginner Tarot student, your choice of Tarot card games is the key to a successful understanding of the messages that the cards offer. It is important to find a tarot package that fits your style and personality and makes you comfortable. Some decks like Minchiate Tarot have additional cards that are not best for beginners but are an exception. As a Tarot novice, you will always have to choose in terms of beautiful Tarot game full of symbolism, so the problem is less to find a great set of tarot cards and more choose only one.

Eclectic Tarot

This page is probably the most comprehensive directory of tarot decks available for free online. While some of the more modern decks might not be there, it's a great place to shop for Windows Tarot deck suitable for beginners. This site also has a lot of tips and tutorials on the Tarot and its history, and it is a great free resource for your Tarot related questions. With over 1200 tarot and Oracle decks reviewed, and more added every day, you'll have plenty of starter tarot packages to choose from.

Llewellyn Worldwide

Llewellyn is an international new age publisher and has a huge collection of tarot games, books, and individual decks with beautiful artwork. You can browse some of the cards in many decks, and even get a free Tarot reading using a selection of them, which can be great if you try to figure out whether you connect with the specific symbolism of a deck or not.

Beetle

Scarabeo is an Italian publisher of tarot cards and books, among other topics related to divination, and their modern website offers a look at their extensive collection of tarot cards. They have a whole collection dedicated to tarot sets, which include introductory books with the bridge. If you are in the Gothic style artwork, they have several modern bridges inspired by fantastic creatures, such as fairies, mermaids, and vampires.

Choosing A Tarot Game For Beginners

There are no strict rules on that Tarot Cards are better to know about tarot cards, but many people will recommend easier decks near to the original tarot decks, than more modern with non-traditional card names or extra cards. However, it is important to choose a package that suits your personality, and many tarot readers will buy only those packages that I personally find beautiful or somehow attract. Navigate until you find a bridge that forces you to buy and use it to take your first steps into the Tarot world.

Tarot Through the Ages

Tarot, pictures, we are more familiar with today, evolved from the genre, board games, played in the 15th century in Italy, and it became popular throughout Europe over the next four centuries.

To thoroughly explore the history of Tarot, you can read Michael Dummet's great book, " The Game of Tarot: From Ferrara to Salt Lake City "(Duckworth, 1980). Dummet, a highly esteemed British philosopher, is the author of many books on tarot cards. His Tarot scholarship is extensive and provides much of the research available at the beginning of the Tarot deck and its variations.

Tarot originally was fun in the classroom for leisure, those with time and money to spend on games. I am sure that at that time, the cards were handmade and illustrated by artists, and each set would vary with the artist's individual representation of the card images. Especially from the 15th up to the 18th century in Europe, variations of tarot games were very popular and enjoyed by people of little wealth and intellect, very similar to chess or bridge. The Tarot of 1700 was a total madness throughout the continent.

There are several decks of tarot cards that have come to represent a familiar iconography, each with its own history, interpretation, and devotees. 15th-century Italian bridge Visconti-Sforza is probably the oldest surviving bridge of this era, with original cards in the collections of several museums around the world. These beautiful artistic images are often reproduced.

And the 19th-century version from the south of France, known as the Tarot of Marseille, is a very popular deck in Europe.

In the US, The Rider-Waite-Smith Tarot deck is most often used today. It was conceived by the well-known Tarot authority A. email. Waite, and published in 1902 by Ryder Co., the simplified graphic style of this deck retains the historical symbolism of previous decks, but seems to be fresh and accessible to modern sensibilities.

Other tarot scholars are convinced that Tarot has its roots even earlier. They see relationships with the Kabbalah, or with ancient Egyptian hieroglyphs. Cards, for games or prophecies, were used in China centuries before they found their way to Europe in the 14th century, and it can be the original embodiment of the Tarot.

It is more likely that Tarot cards were brought to Europe through card games that were popular in the Old World Of Arabia. In France in the 18th Century, Antoine Court De Gebelin promoted the concept that Tarot cards came from mystical practices in ancient Egypt, which is described in his multi-volume work, Le Monde Primitif. Another Frenchman, Etteillla, is considered the first to recreate the tarot as a "divination" device. Basically, it is the first tarot reader. Reproductions of his book Thoth Tarot and other publications of Etteilla are still available today.

Tarot Reading turned out to be a new construction during the embrace of the Victorian age of spiritualism and occultism, laying the foundation for what would become the Tarot of the New Age School we know today.

There is an extensive scholarship and research on the history of tarot cards, either from online sources or in libraries, for those interested in exploring the topic. But for most of us, the story is not as convincing as the question of how Tarot makes sense in our lives.

Steps To Giving a Great Tarot Reading

Becoming a good Tarot reader requires much more than remembering the meaning of tarot cards and knowing tarot cards. Reading tarot requires practice, patience, and, most importantly, the willingness to trust your own intuition. If you are reading for yourself or someone else, there are some very useful procedures to ensure good reading.

1. Prepare a quiet environment

Believe it or not, the environment in which you run and read tarot cards can significantly affect the reading. Not only can the environment affect you as a tarot reader, but it can also have consequences for the person being read. When reading tarot cards, it is always important to postpone your personal problems and fears. Creating a comfortable space to help you stay focused and calm will help you stay objective and neutral while reading. Rituals like lighting candles or burning incense can also help you get in the mood.

2. Choose a meaningful map

When reading tarot cards, significant cards serve as a representation of the person being read or the situation asking. If you use the card-marking to represent the reading in person, most of the readers of Tarot cards tend to use the court cards either by associating the physical attributes of the researcher with one of the court cards or by a combination of their astrological sign to one of the court cards. If you choose and the Access Map has a specific situation, you can be creative as you like. Depending on the severity of the application, you can choose a map of the main arcane or smaller arcane. Major arcane cards tend to be used for major environmental issues, while less obscure cards tend to focus on everyday concerns.

Meaningful maps will also help you stay focused on the person you are reading. In many tarot cards, this means that the cards are located in the center. Help the tarot reader interpret and help him identify the key questions that lie around the interviewer.

3. Choosing the right course of Tarot

Tarot decks are the layout of cards arranged in a certain scheme. Each location of the map in the range has a specific meaning. When individual Tarot Cards are assembled for the spread of tarot cards, their meanings can be used to create a kind of story. The Tarot reader then interprets the cards according to their position and the relationships between them at the bow.

As a tarot reader, it is important to choose the spread of Tarot, which corresponds to the question asked. If the question is, for example, about love, then you probably want to enjoy the spread of love. In some cases, it is recommended to create your own spread of tarot cards. This can be especially useful when it comes to more than one topic.

4. Formulation of questions

The way the interviewer frames or asks a question before reading it can have a significant effect on the overall usefulness of reading. The more accurate the interviewer with his question, the more likely it is that reading tarot cards will solve their problem in a particular way. It is also useful to put an end to this question. Open questions can reveal hidden or overlooked questions that would otherwise have been overlooked. Open questions can also help the tarot reader discover the main problems or other influences that can affect the person reading them.

5. Mixing Boards

There are several approaches to mixing cards before tarot reading. This is usually the point where you have to actually read touch the card (although some tarot readers don't want anyone to manipulate their cards). If you decide to leave the investigator to manipulate the cards, you need to make sure that they are responsible, focusing on how to mix so that this energy can be transferred to the card. There are also several approaches to the "cutting" of paper, among the most popular are that the interviewer cuts the bridge three times with his left hand.

6. How do I know your tarot pack?

Before giving tarot reading, I always encourage people to give them time to really know the Tarot game that will work. This will help you not only to get acquainted with the cards, but also to deepen the understanding of their importance and mutual interconnection in the spread of tarot. Inevitably, those who receive and read tarot cards as they will, always take your relationship with their own cards. If you do not know the game with which you work, it is likely to come when reading tarot cards.

Things You Didn't Want to Know About Tarot

Do you love tarot cards because of its aura of mystery, esoteric history, or magical qualities? If you think that Tarot Cards are peculiar because of one of these reasons, you will not like what I have to say in this book.

I will look at the real history of Tarot, and my research on it has led me to conclusions that are different from what most of you have read online, and may be different from the one that wants you to believe are the facts behind Tarot.

I enjoy using tarot cards for over 25 years, and I love tarot symbology and tarot divination. Still, I don't like it when uninformed people create a romantic/mystical fantasy story for these cards.

I collected the first ten pieces of information that I think tarot readers need to know about the origins of Tarot. These data were collected by art historians, map collectors, and my research in museums and libraries.

Number 1

For those of you who like the idea that Tarot Cards are a magical or mystical instrument that has been handed down since the Egyptian or even the Atlantis era, I'm sorry, but there is absolutely no evidence of that. Not only is there no evidence, but when you look at the first known tarot cards and look at how they were born, there is not even a possibility of connection with Egypt or the mythical Atlantis. I hear you say, "But I've seen maps that have Egyptian drawings or symbols on them!" And you might have, but these are subsequent additions to the work of Tarot, and the images on which the Tarot is based on do not have Egyptian drawings or symbols.

The First Surviving Tarot Cards are hand-painted decks that were made in Italy, around the year 1441. They were made for the Court of Filippo Maria Visconti, Duke of Milan (from 1412 to 1447), and these cards are known as Visconti-Sforza Tarot. This name was given to them because it was the name of the families for which these cards were created. We know this because the heraldry of these families was included in the maps themselves. Representations of family members are also used in Maps.

Number 2

It has been claimed that today's ordinary playing cards are derived from tarot cards. The Joker is a representative of the card of the Madman of the major Arcans. Sorry, but ordinary playing cards developed much earlier and entered Europe from the Islamic world around 1375.

Number 3

The combinations of tarot cards, as we know them, are very different from the original ones. Tarot costumes derive from Islamic playing cards that were coins, cups, swords, and Polo sticks. The game of polo was very important in Islamic culture, but it was not known in Europe when the cards arrived, so the suit of Polo sticks became known as the suit of sticks or sticks. In Italy and Spain, playing cards preserved the costumes of batons, coins, cups, and swords.

Number 4

Tarot costumes, as we know them, have evolved from these Islamic playing cards, and various occultists over the years have changed the original costumes to make the Tarot more magical or mysterious. Sticks/sticks/slats were changed to chopsticks, and the costume of coins was changed to Pentacles.

Number 5

For many years, there was a theory that gypsies brought tarot cards to Europe, and this notion, unfortunately, became an accepted "fact" in the history of tarot cards. However, we know that the Gypsies arrived in Western Europe in 1417, but playing cards were known in Catalonia, a region of northeastern Spain, in 1370, so the cards arrived 47 years earlier than the Gypsies. And in historical documents, gypsies are called only palm readers; they are not talked about using cards for divination until 1891. And even then, the cards they refer to are standard playing cards, not Tarot Cards.

Number 6

Tarot cards were not intended as a means of hiding esoteric information from ignorant or invasive Nations. There are many references to tarot during the 15th century, and all refer to tarot as a game. It is never mentioned as having been used in any other form during this period. It was conceived as a game and no esoteric connection, nor divinatory properties, was attributed to it until several centuries later. The most likely reason for his invention was that the Duke of Milan (Filippo Maria Visconti) wanted a variation on the standard playing card set he had used. He asked his artist Bonifacio Bembo to create an extension of this game.

Number 7

The images of cards in modern Tarot Cards are similar in some respects to the original tarot cards created by Bembo, but there have been some changes. Over the years, images on maps have been modified by occultists to make them more magical or mysterious. A good example of these changes is the card known as the fool. Rather than being shown as a naive and confident soul who dragged through the countryside with his faithful dog, he was originally depicted in rags, looking quite miserable. He was considered the weakest of all in the physical field. It was the classic "village idiot." The charter called the High Priestess was known as the Popess. The heiress was once called the Pope. The Hermit was known as the hunchback or the father. The Hanged Man was the traitor, and the judgment was known as the Angel.

Number 8

The main Arcane maps are based on Christian principles, not on esoteric or magical knowledge. For the major Arcanes, the artist, Bembo, decided to use an allegory of religious teachings that could easily be displayed in a series of images. If you look at the sources of the XV and XVI centuries and some of the first bridges that list the elements in a sequence, you will see a separate model emerge. This model shows the physical kingdom as the lowest form of existence, and then shows the path of Christian spirituality leading to their God. The last map of the Greater Arcane is the map of the world, and one of the first authors on the subject described this last map, as "the world," which is God the father. The terms "major arcane" and "minor arcane" are relatively recent terminology. Paul Christian, an occultist of the 1800s, introduced these terms in the Tarot. Again, these terms were given to tarot cards to make it more magical and mysterious. The word Arcana means mysterious or secret, and by granting the cards these Latin titles, it was imbued with a mystical quality that was never wanted by the original designers of the game.

Number 9

Some occultists believe that there is a direct link between the 22 ways of the Cabal and the major Arcanes. Pico della Mirandola was responsible for introducing the Cabal to Western occultists. Still, he did so more than 40 years after the existence of the Tarot cards, so the tarot images were certainly not based on or related to this Hebrew alphabet and magic system. If the cabalists had invented tarot cards, the first cards had Hebrew letters on them; and they would not have used images such as death or the devil, or photos of women on them. Jewish Kabbalists did not like images of this nature, nor those of the human form, because they were forbidden by the first commandment which constituted "cut images." And on the contrary, tarot cards do not appear in any way in kabbalistic literature. Tarot cards do not descend from Jewish culture, and Jewish cabalists today do not recognize tarot cards as part of their beliefs.

Any meaning between the Tarot and the Cabal is the result of four main things;

1) the occultists conveniently hid some basic ideas about the Cabal to better fit their theory about a game between the two subjects. For example, papers such as the Pope and The Last Judgment are obviously Christian, not Jewish.

2) when designing a Tarot deck, occultists often implanted additional symbols inside the Tarot card images to satisfy the Cabal. For example, Levi introduced on the magician's table the signs of the "elementary" suit to prove that this card represented "First matter" - the elements are the basis from which all things were composed.

3) occultists often organized the order of cards to better fit their theories. The Golden Dawn exchanged Justice and strength to conform to the Jewish letters and correspondents.

4) with archetypal images such as tarot cards, it is not too difficult to see an esoteric system as similar to another system.

In 1778 Court De Gébelin and Count de Mellet were the first to suggest a link between the Tarot and the Cabal, and this was collected and expanded by Lévi, an occultist with dubious research skills. But because of Levi's high reputation in the magical world of that era, the association between Tarot and Cabal was simply considered a fact from that moment on, without anyone worrying about whether he was right or not.

Number 10

Elementary associations with the four seeds are another subsequent invention of the occultists and are not part of the original concept of tarot cards. Eliphas Lévi gave to Tarot the associations that are still accepted in most Tarot books today: batons / wands = fire; coins / Pentacles = Earth; cups = water; Swords = air.

Conclusion: tarot evolution is an information puzzle with pieces from scattered directions, and is derived from many cultures and many minds.

When you think about tarot cards, I would like you to remember that there are two main types of tarot decks, and they are very far apart from each other. We have historical Tarot, which was simply designed as a card game, and now we have modern Tarot, which was derived from and evolved from historical Tarot. The first tarot cards do not have mystical or magical qualities associated with it. The historical Tarot was an invention of the 15th century and was based on the cultural and historical and religious expressions of its time-nothing more, nothing less.

Modern Tarot has esoteric and mystical associations, but only because it was placed there in recent centuries, not because it is related to some ancient source of secret knowledge. To write all this, I'm not trying to belittle the Tarot or its heritage. I'm just trying to add a rational voice to the irrational accounts that some people think of passing as the "story" of tarot cards.

Modern Tarot has become a powerful set of mystical images that can legitimately be seen as a spiritual journey. It is full of magical, esoteric symbols and archetypes, making it a playground for the imagination. That's great! This is an important part of the place of the Tarot in today's world. However, when people promote a fictional story simply to heighten a subject's mystique, it undermines the value of its true nature when the truth is finally revealed.

The true history of the evolution of the Tarot is just as interesting as the factories. The original version may not look as magical or mysterious as its counterpart, but it is still fascinating. When you see an article that tells about the "mysterious and dark" origins of tarot cards, please delve deeper; you will find that the author did not bother to do serious research on the subject.

Tarot Cards for Beginners

While tarot cards can pale to play a normal deck, enjoying a whopping seventy-eight different cards, any beginner can get a pack and start practicing if they understand the fundamentals. The cards in the tarot pack can be divided into several categories:

Adapt

Main and smaller Arcanes

Pip Card

Court Documents

Once you understand the different characteristics of any category, reading tarot cards is simply a matter of mixing and matching information.

The most basic distribution of Tarot Cards is between the twenty-two main Arcanes, forty pip cards, and sixteen Court cards. The best way to begin to understand the meaning of each card is to arrange each of the 22 main Arcana in a circle, with the first card in position twelve. From there, looking through the map clockwise, you will be able to follow the path of the soul inevitably passes during its existence.

Around the first circle, then place forty pip cards. It begins with a Pentacles suit, the first twelve-position map depicting the winter solstice. In the position of three, follow the Pentacles suit with a sword suit, indicating the spring equinox. Then place the wand suit in a six-hour position, which means the summer solstice. Finally, it ends with a suite of Cups, starting with the position of the nine and marking the autumn equinox. Just as the rotation of the main Arcana represents a cycle, the rotation of the PIP map demonstrates the movement of the Earth around the sun through the seasons.

Finally, between these two circles, evenly distribute the remaining sixteen Court cards, working from the princess to the king in the seeds that correspond to the outer circle. These maps show different important personalities and how we grow over the years.

In this exercise, it is important to note that just because one card fell into the upper circle or the lower part is not more important than the other. Each card, whether it's major arcana or Minor Arcana, has a very special place in tarot reading.

Each seed in a smaller Arcane has very specific meanings that play an integral role in reading.

Cups: the cups are connected to the water element. Just as water can flow smoothly, be stopped by the dam, or boil and anger in the storm, as well as our emotions. When reading the cards that fall under the cups, it is important to read the procedure from one to ten in an emotional way.

Chopsticks: the chopsticks are attached to the fire element. Fire full of rhythm and movement; it can create and destroy. Therefore, chopsticks are the germ of change and action. Reading this dress, you will see cards that represent the first steps in a new beginning, the creation of our destiny, and cards that tell us that we acted too quickly, without thinking about the future.

Pentacle: Pentacles are associated with the element earth. The Earth is stable, solid, grounded. This is where we build our homes, feed ourselves, and support ourselves. Similarly, these dresses focus on the body and our senses. Whether it's creating a family environment where you feel safe, getting financial security, or taking care of yourself and building a family, all this will be found, if you read the pentacles.

Swords: swords are connected to the air element. We can't live without air, and we can't breathe. However, the air can also take your breath away in an instant. Just as the air can be sharp and pungent, so can the sword. This dress focuses on the intellect. It was said that there is no greater weapon than words, so beware of the warning that this seed can carry in terms of communication with others. It also explores the need for mental clarity and new ideas.

It also takes into account the personalities represented in the court's documents. These cards are incredibly important in reading because they can be directly related to you or someone who is closely related to your situation. Sometimes, it can help us understand who we can turn to for help, or who could hinder our progress.

Princesses: princesses and pages are interchangeable, and your deck will certainly be one or the other, but never both. When you draw a princess, you read about someone who is somehow young. Perhaps they have unfulfilled and unrecognized potential or are, in fact, a child. A princess can mean a student or someone who has just started a new adventure in her life.

Princes: princes are synonymous with Knights in a tarot reading, and again the bridge will have one or the other, but never both. The principles symbolize movement and action; they thirst for progress in life and can often be naively idealistic. People who are read like a prince are warned about actions without thinking because they often jump the gun and assume that everything will work out in the best case. Princes are considered eager in all things and are a generous type of person who is always eager to help others.

Queens are considered caring and intuitive people. They are highly respected and admired and lead inspiration rather than command. The Queen can represent a man or a woman if it is someone who illustrates the above aspects. Often, they are a mature person or a relative- someone with life experience to draw on when offering advice.

Kings represent a person who grew up in his life and is now wise and perfect. Often the person who is represented by this card will feel a great duty and responsibility towards others, placing the needs of friends and family before their own.

After examining the classifications of court cards, seeds, and how to arrange a set of tarot cards in order to trace its history, the meaning of each card should begin to become clear. At this time, a beginner could choose a deck card and give it at least a very simple definition. Once you feel comfortable with this information, consider the numbers from one to ten and finally go through all the main mysterious cards one by one. When you have an understanding of what each number represents, and what the titles of the major arcanes represent, you can then read tarot de Marseille. It will take practice, and sometimes, you may need to refer to the reference table, but slowly and surely understand the concepts that go into the divisions of tarot cards, and everyone can pick up and be a simple and basic tarot reader.

Make your Own Tarot Card Deck

A Tarot card game is something that many people want to use, but I do not know which formula to choose. The number of tarot games available can be surprising to some. And while you might like a few tarot card games, you may not be able to afford more than one. Instead of wasting time looking at the tarot decks available, it's time to make your own tarot deck exactly to your specifications.

You will need some supplies before making a tarot pack for you. To begin with, you need a thicker quality paper on which you can make drawings of Tarot. If you find a paper with a pattern on one side and an empty area on the other, everything is better. Take this paper and cut it into 78 corresponding squares or rectangles, to your liking. Then collect artistic needs to create drawings on the empty side of the paper. Things like markers and colored pencils are ideal because they do not rub.

If you want to imitate the ideas of a traditional tarot card pack, you will want to look for a real tarot card pack or a card online. This way, you can start with an idea for each card, but you can create your own unique patterns. Look at the examples of tarot as simply inspiration; it does not have pictures that you need to copy. For example, you can make a five-stroke, but the chopsticks can look as you like, and there may be other background images you call.

Finally, to complete the package, you need to create a safe place to stay when it is not in use. You can buy a box or bag that can be used to store your cards, for example. And then you can decorate this box or bag to help you make this room something more personal and special. Some people also choose to laminate their cards to add a layer of protection and stability.

Regardless of your reasons for wanting a tarot, remember that you do not need to spend a lot of money or even adhere to "traditional" models. To see the future, you can start with the cards created by your own hands.

How to Predict the Future Using a Tarot Deck

Is it possible to predict the future? What about the Tarot deck? Yes, it is! Read on, and you'll find out how.

Extract your favorite tarot pack or fortune teller. It is better to stay in a quiet space, but the most important thing is to work with cards. All these are amazing tools that can help create a contemplative atmosphere. It works best with a tarot card or Oracle decks, asking open questions rather than yes/no questions. Some open question tips are listed below. Yes/no question would be how to tear off daisy's petals, "does she love me? Or don't you like me?"I have a raise."

What kind of energy will I have to monitor in July?

My annual exam is scheduled for the last week of March. What areas of improvement will be discussed in my review?

I'm going to propose to my girlfriend. What is the most favorable Week and day to ask her?

My son is starting a new school. What energy do we need to know about his school? Will the change make him succeed?

Tomorrow is Monday, what kind of energy do I meet at work? House? On the highway?

Take your time, formulate, and explore each question. Make sure the question is exactly what you want to know. Vague questions will give you vague and often frustrating answers. An example of a vague question can be: "why can't I find a good job? Instead, you might ask, "What kind of energy do I have to get a better job?"

After formulating and considering your question on the day you wanted education, take the Tarot platform (or Oracle platform). Mix the cards and think about your question. Download the map. Meditate on the map. Note the story that the map tells you or the story that makes you think. It could be Little Red Riding Hood, or Uncle Ted came across a piece of wildflower. History does not matter, neither real nor fictitious. Look at the colors and what they represent for you. Look at the numbers, the time, the symbols you see on the maps. Do not forget about the traditions of Tarot meanings.

During meditation, focus on the map of the symbol, shape, or color that represents the shapes of the map. Let the shape, symbol, color dance in your head until you form the next one. In the calendar, write it or draw it and all other information you received. Do not judge the information that comes. Write down what it is. The image of a ship sinking in the Blood Red Sea may not mean a real wreck. It could be a prediction that the 15th day In January of next year, the company you work for may have a huge drop in the price of their shares and are left in the red financially. Pay attention to everything, regardless of whether it makes sense or not.

To what extent it is necessary to request information in the future. If you want to know about next week or about seven months in the future, it doesn't matter. Tradition says not to ask more than six months in advance, because the energy around the event, the person, etc. can change. However, the same applies to any reading. Two hours later, energy could change for up to two decades in the future.

If you have received forecast-based information, you should consider reconnecting to maps a week or a month before the forecast date. People change their minds, learn new skills, and someone may die, they can become all sorts of things that can affect time. Whether something changes or not, you have a strong answer. If things are completely different, you can find out what new energies will affect that day.

Be vigilant for cards, labels, symbols, colors, etc. that are repeated in each of your predictive data. The more something is repeated, the more news it is.

If you read about other people, pay attention to the repetition in the cards; if you see one or more cards, it repeats again and again, regardless of the person reading. This occurs mainly for four to six months. Attention. If a map of the tower appears at each reading, this could mean another collapse of the bank. If the moon appears, it could mean that we have an emotional turn for the event. In either case, a map or not a map, this repetition means that change is coming. Something is happening socially, politically, or economically.

Start predicting your future, pull up the calendar, or turn on the phone. Extract any tool to maintain a normal life. Using tarot cards or Oracle decks, you can predict the future.

RWS Tarot - A Brief Introduction

The Rider Waite Smith Tarot deck is probably the most popular and well known of all tarot decks that are available today. The name comes from William RIDER & son-the original editor, Arthur Edward WAITE-the academic and mystic who commissioned the creation of this game, and Pamela Colman SMITH-the talented but often neglected artist, who drew pictures from the Rider-Waite Tarot game (as it is often called). Waite and Smith were both members of the Order of Golden Dawn, the famous but fleeting occult group of the 19th century.

RWS tarot card game was released in 1909 and was the first widely available game with illustrated minor arcane cards. Fifty-six tiny arcane cards, also known as "pecks," today had a wealth of symbolism displayed in the pictures, as well as twenty-two major mysterious cards. Until then, less mysterious cards on the tarot deck showed only four cups, or six chopsticks or eight swords. RWS tarot cards with illustrated "pips," as well as evocative images of the main Arcana, finally revolutionize the world of tarot cards. When Waite designed his tarot package, he maintained a basic sequence of cards, even as he changed card numbering and fairness in the main Arcanes. There is debate about who actually designed the minor Arcane cards. It was said that Waite designed and gave Smith full instructions or just told her your thoughts and gave free rein to their artistic talents to create images. Each card carries a monogram of Pamela Colman Smith, usually in one of the lower corners.

The original print of the albums was tragically destroyed in the London bombing, and the release ended. In 1971, US Games Inc. he began publishing a protected fax version of the game.

These days, many bridges follow the basic pattern of the RWS tarot deck. There are RW versions that were re-colored, but kept on designs of this original line. Versions that have been redesigned usually have the same basic numbers and parameters on maps with similar symbolism. Game type RWS is generally recommended for beginners, because the basic visual scenes may be more easily associated with keywords, to make it easier to memorize and understand the meaning of each card. However, there are also many experienced readers whose favorite reading platform is an RWS or variant. Most books for beginners and beginners use illustrations of the RWS bridge for learning purposes.

One thing is certain, if Arthur Edward Waite and Pamela Colman Smith didn't have to work together to create a tarot deck-RWS tarot would be very different from what we are accustomed to today.

Waite Tarot - Information About Waite Tarot

Waite Tarot is one of the most popular existing card games. Card reading has been around for a long time. People turn to the prediction of the future to get answers to their most desired questions. In 1909, A. email. Waite created his famous cards and was issued by the rider company, thus getting the name of The Rider-Waite Tarot card. There are a lot of articles about tarot cards and reading outside, so I'll talk about the meaning of the inverted card.

Each time, when the player mixes cards, some of them end upside down; for beginners, it is recommended to ignore it and turn it in the right direction. Once the newcomer has gained experience, he should start paying attention to the inverted card. Everyone knows that each Waite Tarot card symbolizes certain energy, and when the reading of the Cards is carried out, the energy collection gives the answer to the researcher. It is commonly known that cards collect energy when mixed and cut. Energy is of a different nature; some are strong, others are weak, others stay in your life, some leaves, as the energies are distributed, you decide the exact situation.

Every time you act on a vertical card, then its energy is free to manifest itself, the characteristics, which contains the Waite Tarot card, are readily available and active, but when we deal with inverted cards, the energy is not fully developed. It can be considered that it is in the early stages or loses energy, is incomplete, or even unavailable. The features of these maps are present, but they cannot be expressed completely.

It is a good idea that you keep track of how many cards you deal vertically and how many upside down. If most Cards are straight, then your energies are free and strong. In this case, the purpose is clear. If the opposite happens, then you have little energy, and the goal is tarnished. If energies are not freely developed, they go wherever they want.

Waite Tarot Cards are a great tool for contact with the energies around us. Life is an endless flow of energy; when a person understands this flow and uses it creatively, then anything will be possible. We should not pretend that inverted cards add a different aspect of your value, and this helps you better interpret Waite Tarot cards.

Tarot Cards Spread

Tarot Cards are distributed differently depending on the questions you want to find answers to. The spread of the Celtic cross is popular because it responds to many aspects, including the current condition of the person, past events, affecting the present, and a possible future that may or may not occur. Dissemination of reports is another common spread, and it reveals the current status of her report, the way the message is controlled, and what aspects of the report should be considered.

Other spreads include astrological, Planetarium, Tetraktys, Cross and Triangle, Mandala, star guide, Tree of life, past, life, and dream spread.

For centuries, people depended on reading tarot cards and palms to predict future events. Gifted persons carried out these data for a fee. The practice is still present in today's modern world, and many people still consult the reader. The beliefs of those who go for reading vary greatly. Some believe in an unchanging fate and use the information to prepare themselves to face everything that happens to them.

Others use the information to make the right choice. These people and entrepreneurs usually occupy positions of responsibility. They want to know the consequences of their actions and the impact of their decisions on their performance. Despite the goals of physical reading, practice is gaining great popularity in society.

What tarot cards are on the market

Many types of tarot cards are available on the market. When mixed, form a pattern on the surface, such as a table. The template is tarot spreads, and each tarot reader has its favorite templates. As with many professions, when a new person begins to work, he must start with simple basic tasks. New Tarot readers should start with simple tarot cards. Deviations differ in the number of cards in the range. Simple deviations include five to one card. The rest includes between six and all cards in the tarot package.

What determines the deviations of the tarot card

The type of spread of tarot cards depends on the questions to which the client wants to answer. Some popular models are suitable for certain questions, and depending on the specific needs of the customer. Reading tarot cards is not difficult to read. The requirement of the reader is the concentration and ability to interpret the meaning of different patterns of Tarot multiplication. This requires great cognitive abilities and memorizing skills.

The simplest scatter is the scatter of three cards. The player mixes the deck, then divides it into three piles. Then the reader takes the card from each pile and puts it on the table with his face. The reader should keep the question in mind during all these activities and focus on the answer. The map on the left side of the tray presents a history question, while the map in the center is associated with the current events surrounding the question. The last card on the right represents the possible future of the problem.

Another extension of tarot cards for beginners is the spread of tarot cards with four cards. To interpret this, the reader mixes the cards with the question in mind. Then the player takes four cards from the top of the deck and spreads them on the table face down and from left to right. The first tarot card from left to right represents the past, the second present, and the third Future of the application. The fourth card is the answer to the question.

Tarot Myth Busters

The purpose of this book is to try to clarify obsolete and unnecessary superstitions related to reading Tarot cards.

Ask all experienced and ethical readers of tarot cards, if they believe that tarot cards are bad, the work of the devil, and only psychics and clairvoyants can read them, they can leave with a laugh. I would have done the same thing. The more I use and work with these cards, the more I understand their true meaning and capabilities.

When using cards with a group of people who claim to have no knowledge of tarot cards, it is always fascinating to hear the answer when the death card spins. A strong hold of breath is, to put it mildly, a whisper: "Oh, death!'. Everyone was sitting at the table, do not mislead us, that I really did not understand the death map; they were led to believe the wrong meaning for this map and more. Then what happens is that eventually, I will explain the correct meaning and convince them of this fact, with the impression that they prefer the drama of the original meaning.

Most cards are made of wood pulp and Printing Ink, created in card shapes with an image on one side and a pattern on the back, all 78 cards. Which is exactly what they are and everything they will ever be. Even digital images are just a display of the image of symbols and works of art. It is the meaning that is the most interesting part.

Tarot has evolved over the centuries, with their history perhaps starting from 15 playing cards. A century, maybe even earlier. Their development as a divination tool is not very clear, but many use a lot of elements as a tool in the future, including; throwing animal bones, chicken entrails, throwing dice, runes, consuming drugs from plants, looking into a bowl of water, plus the elegant art of drinking cup, sometimes I used cappuccino foam and I know beer is used too.

Hollywood is also responsible for many myths today; the meaning of the devil's map has been edited so that it is abused to show the real death in the film. It is a cheap supplement to add atmosphere and fear. Tarot readers are depicted as the mysterious companion, dressed in flowing clothes, with turbans, excessive jewelry, and bad taste; actors are without exception depicted as gypsy fortune-tellers in a tent or caravan with a crystal ball on the table. It's about showcases and hammers.

Superstition around the Tarot is a work of fiction, perhaps built by people who want to add mystery and control; they can fabricate an idea that they have special mastery, secret knowledge, and gifts. It is an attraction to hide their insecurity. If the tarot reader is good, he has nothing to prove, word of mouth will be enough. The wardrobe of unusual clothes is the last thing that a decent Tarot card needs to increase its reputation.

Most superstitions are quite recent, in the last century, gained momentum with the advent of cinema, television, and a significant increase in the number of people interested in Tarot. These myths also increased in volume and were heavily embroidered along the way.

We distract the most popular:

You should never buy your own tarot cards.

If that were the case, I would still be waiting for my first card game. I don't know why or where it started; it doesn't make sense. This is a very good thing, who else will know exactly what style of cards you like or "talk?" Enjoy looking at the different styles in bookstores and online, ask to see friends, maps, valuable research, and collection of different Tarot decks. In the end, you can design your own.

Never Let Others Touch Your Tarot Cards.

I understand that someone is very special and does not like all Tom, Dick, or Harry to manipulate your cards, but nothing bad will happen if others touch your deck. I've been using the same board for over 12 years, and it made me proud, when someone asks to look at their cards, they often expect me to refuse, but I'm happy to go on and explain a little bit about them. I'll stir it up. This is the perfect time to ask questions and clarify some myths.

Only fortune tellers can read tarot cards.

Yes, clairvoyants can read tarot cards, especially if they have studied them, and the same applies to everyone, we can all read them. Some people understand the cards and can read them without any exercise, but most of us will have to work. Is it possible that we all learned to read tarot cards, whether we have the right books, or/and an online course, another tarot card, which teaches us how; we all need a place to start. Enriches tarot reading, if the reader is psychic, clairvoyant and/or intuitive, there are professional readers, who do not qualify for any of the previous characteristics, but studied and practiced, until he becomes more than competent.

The purpose of this article is to try to clarify the obsolete and unnecessary superstitions associated with reading Tarot cards.

The above answer also applies to doctors, psychologists, police officers, military, and people in business, you know, they read maps. There is a package for everyone; hundreds of tarot styles, from Egyptian Arthurian, fairies, Lord of the Rings; go online and see for yourself. Outside, someone is working on their own deck of cards. There is also someone out there looking for enlightenment, advice, inner wisdom as they shuffle their tarot cards. It's for everyone. Why do witches have fun?

Tarot Cards are magical.

No, absolutely not. They are manufactured, packaged, and shipped wholesale or stored. I'm sorry if I ruined everything for you. They are used as a reading tool, symbols, meanings, and images that trigger the flow of information. Look at them as they are and avoid myths.

Tarot Cards are bad.

Tarot cards do not have magical properties or bad qualities; they are just Cards. All decent Tarot readers will use the cards to help, enlighten, show alternative options, answer questions, in a variety of good and useful ways. They would never have thought of doing it differently. Anyone who claims to use them for evil purposes is mistaken and deceives others.

We have not heard of the cards accused of wrongdoing.

The Gypsies Invented The Tarot.

There is no evidence that the Gypsies played a role in the development of tarot cards. Tarot has evolved from a deck of cards to the 15th century or earlier, in Europe, with the use of expensive, hand-painted gifts ordered by aristocrats, to serially produced woodcuts for the public to buy.

Tarot Cards Are Never Wrong.

Tarot Cards are used to illuminate the paths and options you have in your life, options, and alternatives. The future is not in the stone, but the sand, it's up to you, the future of the road you take, there may be a little more detours along the road, you will probably end up in the same place. Free will and choice to play an important role in your life and tarot cards can reflect this.

Tarot Cards Come From Egypt

These rumors and scams began with the trial of Gebelin. He misinterpreted two Egyptian words, believing that they had an average Tarot, and it was only when the rosette Stone was translated after 1799 that his error was clear.

Tarot cards cannot be read by phone

Of course, they can, it is as simple as the client asks the question, and the Tarot reader then writes the question, shuffles the cards and continues to read. This also applies to reading on the internet; this is the same technique. Just because this person, the querent, is not sitting next to you, does not mean that you cannot interact and give them answers with the help of tarot cards. Sometimes, I would type the answer and print it or email it, and it's just as valid.

Cats Will Undermine Your Skill.

When it was first suggested, my jaw took. Needless to say, I invited the four cats in the family to read that night. God knows where it started. That is not a piece of truth.

Pregnant Women Should Not Read Cards

If this were true, health warnings would be printed on the sides of card packs. It is absolutely safe for pregnant women to read the cards; they may be able to level the cards on their bump as they do.

You Can't Read Tarot Cards.

Yes, of course, you can, but first, write a question on paper and use a tarot book that you believe for answers. The trick is to use the answer books on the cards for your answer; otherwise, you can find the fight unbiased or detached. By writing all this, you can check so late.

You don't want anyone to read it, and it's a method for development.

Your tarot cards should be wrapped in silk.

Only if you like silk, I use old silk scarves that are loved and difficult to separate; this prevents the edge of the paper from scratches. In addition, it is a joy to the touch. As for my "working" platform, which lives in a gadget bag, usually purchased to protect and carry MP3 players. Two bridges and a digital recorder can fit into it. No one knows what's inside when I wear it.

Tarot Cards Are The Work Of The Devil.

Of course not. They are the work of people who want to help others, help them with the problems they have, improve their lives, discover new techniques for taking responsibility, use modern psychology. Many of these people are professional classes, doctors, psychologists, psychiatrists, nurses, scientists, consultants, etc. what circulates, happens.

The Cards Are Hidden

The word occultism means hidden. We know that the cards came from playing cards in the 15th of the XIX century, with different groups interested in them and attaching their own beliefs and meanings. The word occult has been used over the years, trying to give a false view of their true use and suggesting something wrong.

Death Map Means Death

Simply put, it means change. If you want to change careers and this map will appear in one reading, you can feel a huge sense of relief, depending on whether you know the true meaning. It's a map that filmmakers use to suggest that there will be an evil death without really appreciating what they are doing. Therefore, Tarot readers spend a lot of time reassuring their clients when this card appears. Change.

Not all tarot readers can be trusted

I can be prejudiced if I answer this! Always stick to the word when looking for someone to give you a reading. Any profession can have a charlatan, a cheater, or a woman. Just a little patience and make sure that the Tarot reader is well thought out. If you are reading and you feel very unhappy with the way things are going, make a quick exit. Ideally, you should have a feeling of well-being after reading, a feeling of clarification, do not feel like you are flying blind. Use your instincts.

Reverse Cards Are Always Terrible.

Some people choose not to use inverted cards during the game so that it sticks to 78 vertical meanings. This means you're going to lose another 78 meanings, and some of them are very, very positive. This simply means studying a little more as you learn, I suggest you look at some tarot books on online bookstores that have the best-inverted Tarot meanings. This will expand your knowledge and reading.

Top Ten Myths about Tarot Cards and Tarot Reading

Myth 1 - "Tarot cards can predict the future."

Predicting the future is not difficult; we can all do it. For example, if you know someone who constantly spends more than it earns and pays for it by building up the debts of credit cards, then it is not hard to predict where he's going. Or, if you know someone who is expecting a baby, you can count on experience, accurately predict that they have many months of lack of sleep and fatigue in advance. Tarot cards do a little more. It has centuries of human experience distilled into a simple philosophy and meaning of each paper. Another way of looking at it is to say that the tarot cards do not make precise predictions of the future, simply allow us to catch a glimpse of some of the likely possibilities.

Myth 2 - "tarot cards come from ancient Egypt."

The first that tarot cards can be dated is the 16th century in Italy. There is no evidence that Tarot exists anywhere else in the world. Some people claim that the cards come from India or China, but this is also baseless speculation.

Myth 3 - "Acceptance of the death card means that someone dies."

Likely. The point of the symbolism of the Cards is that they represent deeper truths than life. Taking all the cards literally would lose layers of meaning and intuition. In the case of the death map of the medieval spirit, death represented an inevitable change and often a journey to a better place. The Charter represents change and evolution. However, the possibility that this sometimes means death cannot be ruled out.

Myth 4 - "Reading the pleasure of Tarot in the occultism."

There are many claims that the tarot cards have pagan, witchcraft, or shamanic roots, and some even involve tarot cards in devil worship and satanic rituals. Another common claim is that the tarot cards originated from ancient religions now forgotten. None of this is true. Tarot cards, as already mentioned, originate from medieval Italy, and the predominant cultural context of that time was Christian. The symbolism of the Cards is Christian or Jewish-A New Testament or an old one. The word "occult" means" hidden," so, in this sense, you can say that reading has something to do with magic because you are trying to reveal what is hidden.

Myth 5 - "Reading your cards will bring bad luck."

Professional readers and those experienced with cards know that it is not true, but this is often repeated. This may stem from the fact that Tarot readers avoid reading their cards. Not because she's unlucky, but because she's not effective. A good tarot reading requires three parts; the questioner, the reader, and the bridge. The reader tries to remain objective and reports to the questioner what the cards say, without any bias or desire to hear a specific message. Playing this role for your reading is difficult, if not impossible.

Myth 6 - "You must have a certain psychic ability to read tarot cards."

Most people can learn to read tarot cards to a smaller or larger extent. No psychic power is needed because all wisdom is in Maps and meanings that have been developed over the years. Actually, if we were psychics, why would you use Tarot Cards? Tarot works best when the reader drops his prejudices and feelings on the problem and leaves only the cards to speak.

Myth 7 - "No one should ever worry about their tarot package."

Some interns do not allow anyone else to touch their tarot cards. Even if they read something, they won't let the interview mix the game up on their own. In my experience, this valuable attitude comes from those who want to build themselves, and their platform will be something special. Let me see what you want. This is contrary to the spirit of the Tarot, which promotes open investigation and sharing of understanding. Allowing customers to shuffle cards helps them feel part of the process and focus on the problem in hand.

Myth 8 "Tarot cards can be used to cast spells or perform other people."

Sometimes it is considered that tarot cards can be used to keep things moving rather than predicting. To influence someone's life from afar, for good or evil. It is very far from what cards are actually, which is simple to understand. There is no reason to believe that tarot cards have a different power than intuition. One of the frequent messages based on the tarot data is, in fact, a bad ability that sometimes we have to influence our lives without talking about someone else. Just to give a tarot would probably say: "Get a grip before you try to change others."

Myth 9 - "Different bridges provide different figurines."

It's a little subjective, but not in my experience. Regardless of the bridge, the meanings obtained during the four centuries remain the same. However, different people will refer more strongly to some of the bridges, rather than the other, and the images with which the client is more comfortable to create the best atmosphere for reading. A cynical person may suspect that this myth is multiplied by the creators of bridges.

Myth 10 - "It's dangerous to have too much data on tarot cards."

There is a belief that people who become obsessed with tarot cards and continue to make one after the second reading, you're out of luck, or take a risk, push yourself over the limit. Perhaps it is true that the search for permanent help can be a sign of an impending crisis. These people could still be near the edge. The main thing is that too many tips hurt anyone and lead only to confusion.

Know All About Your Love Life Through Love Tarot Reading

Love and emotions can cloud judgments and leave you confused. It can affect other aspects of your life and get you down.

It is better to clarify issues related to love, relationship, and progress in life.

Tarot provides meaningful answers and directions to define your situation and what you can do to change the situation for the better.

Formulate specific questions and problems before going for a love tarot reading

Interestingly, experienced and gifted Tarot readers first find out what exactly your interest is and what your questions are when you approach them for the love tarot reading.

Then it exposes the number of cards in a template.

In general, you can question classified information as relating to you, love, and your love life in the future, how to find love, how to resolve conflicts, and to spread the love of the couple.

For each type, the medium tarot reader will spread the cards in a special way and invent the love of reading.

Tarot Love Spreads

In a love tarot reading, the reader can take advantage of specific spreads, which usually defines the relationship Tarot deviations, such as finding love to spread, love bottom line spread, relationship deviations, and couple reading deviations. The number of Cards selected can vary from five to twelve.

Your friendly Tarot reader will arrange tarot cards according to the problem. Then each card is read for its individual interpretation and relative to other cards that appear in the span. Each card has a related question. For example, the first card may concern why you are still free. The second card shows you how to overcome this situation, and the third card will inform you about the positive aspect of your potential partner.

An example is the Empress's card. If it happens in your spread and stands, it represents the result, and its symbol is Venus, showing positive developments are in stock in the near future. In itself, it means one thing. The Tarot reader interprets the card, your question, and other cards, and comes up with a detailed answer.

In case the problems with love and relationship bother you, contact the tarot expert to read the Tarot of love.

Knowing your wishes, the Tarot reader will arrange the game in a special way specifically for the love tarot reading session that gives you the long-awaited answers.

Using the Tarot to Find Love

Undoubtedly, the most common survey when reading tarot is about love. It often seems that true love is something that is outside of yourself; it is the external force or the act of Destiny over which we have little control. In fact, the search for love begins with ourselves. Love is a Genesis that manifests itself in our inner beings. A happy and successful relationship begins with ourselves.

The best relationships are those in which both partners find out who they are. When a person develops with a strong sense of self, his partnership will most likely blossom. With self-consciousness, a person is more able to express his feelings and establish appropriate boundaries. They know their own needs and the needs of their partners. Above all, for someone who is single, can recognize the qualities of a potential partner that will work or not.

In the individual tarot tips on Love Matters, Most Tarot readers and psychics tend to focus directly on the current energy of someone's love life. They often do not realize the influence of their own systems of belief or behavior. During a tarot reading, it is really up to the individual to ask the tarot reader or psychic to explore the topic of their level of personal development and how it can affect their love life. A good tarot reader can read it immediately. Love problems must change their orientation. Instead of asking when I would find love? Try to explore the areas that prevent you from finding love. Here are some questions that can be very useful during a love tarot reading.

1. Where are the areas I need to grow to find love?

2. What's keeping me from finding love?

3. What do I need to know about myself so that I can meet a partner?

4. What are my behaviors that affect my love life?

5. What should I think of love?

6. What areas should I change?

7. Where can I not talk?

8. What do I have to do to open myself to love?

The more you learn about yourself, the more likely you will meet the perfect love. It is important to remember that when a person uses tarot for love, tarot serves as a seer. Tarot reading is a tool of self-renewal and growth. In truth, Tarot is a tool that is available to all who wish to explore their own inner workings. This is an incredibly effective method of immersing ourselves in the deepest areas of ourselves that affect our current relationships. Tarot data will never reveal our secrets that remain out of sight.

Tarot reading serves as a guide. They are mirrors that reflect our truths. When it comes to love, tarot cards can lead us to the manifestation of our goals and dreams. They reveal our vulnerabilities and the areas that prevent us from flourishing. In a love tarot card, you can find out what affects us and highlights situations that we may have been aware of. Above all, Tarot offers us a new sense of awareness of who we are. In the end, a tarot reading can open us to love.

As for love, there is nothing like a good tarot reading. Tarot cards offer a unique perspective that illuminates the nature of our relationships. I am here to guide you on your journey, both personally and romantic. Questions about love are by far the most common questions asked when reading the tarot. However, many people are disappointed or dissatisfied. The cause of this is often the questions that are asked. The most important aspect of successful tarot reading is to ask the right questions.

The most common mistake that is made when reading the tarot is the preservation of information. People do this when they question or test the ability of a tarot reader. It is quite normal to worry when working with a new tarot reader, especially if this is the first time you will receive a reading. In these circumstances, the biggest problem is the lack of openness of mind. Unfortunately, you do not need this or that tarot reader. The retention of information can ultimately disrupt the ability of the Tarot reader.

When you get a tarot reading, the best approach is to stay open to your questions about love prepared before you start reading. A professional tarot reader understands the cards and has learned to interpret their meaning. The more accurate you will be with a tarot reader, the better it will be able to help you read. Take the time to justify yourself with doubts and let yourself be guided by the cards. You will be surprised at the amount of information you can receive when you stay recipient.

The best questions to ask at first reading love tarot should not be in black and white. In other words, asking if someone you love or if your relationship will work can give the Tarot reader very little work. Here are some examples of open-ended questions that might be useful when reading Tarot a message.

1. What affects my relationship?

2. What is touching my interest in love now?

3. How could I develop this relationship?

4. What should I understand about myself?

5. What should I understand about my interest in love?

6. What is the potential outcome of this report?

7. What should I do to bring a romantic relationship into my life?

The list can go on, and you can be as creative as you want. Asking carefully planned questions can lead to very rewarding tarot readings.

It is also wise to inform the Tarot reader about the context of your situation. This is especially true for the tarot details of love. By allowing the Tarot reader to fully understand the nature of your situation, the more they will be able to guide you. The history of the situation often improves the Reading of tarot cards. This gives the reader a broader perspective and allows him to understand the problems he is facing. It also lets you know what has affected your relationship.

Finally, it is important to remember that a good Tarot reader will never tell you what to do. They are essentially messengers. You are your master, and you have your free will. You have the power to choose your own paths and behaviors. When it comes to love, you are always the best guide. While tarot readings can often reveal important influences, they still have the power to make their own decisions and choose their own plan of action.

How to Get an Accurate Love Tarot Reading

How do you better read love tarot cards? This is an important question because most people who ask to read love tarot cards end up confused or disappointed after reading it. Yet questions about love, relationships, marriage, divorce, and soul mates remain the most frequently asked questions in reading.

The most common mistake that people make when consulting with a psychic card reader or tarot cards about love and relationships is to keep the information for the purpose of testing the reader. If you are skeptical about tarot cards, do not waste your money reading. This act of non-supply can lead to incorrect values and can be easily confused.

A good love tarot reader will know how to interpret the cards to personalize the reading for the querent before them so that the specific questions that you have about your love and relationships can be specified exactly. Since there are many ways to interpret maps, the more information provided to the reader, the more accurate the reading.

Here's an example. If you want to know if your partner is cheating on you or not, ask this question, rather than "is there another man/woman in his life?" In the life of a man, there are always other women and another man in the life of a woman. Maybe they're not in love. In a love tarot reading, an important person can appear in such cards as a father, brother, close friend.

This does not necessarily mean infidelity. The reader needs some information to interpret the cards specifically to your situation because different cards can have different meanings. The context in which the questions were asked, the placement in the spread of tarot cards, as well as the reader's intuition contribute to getting a good reading of love tarot cards. Be very specific about all the questions you have about your love from the very beginning. If you want to know whether or not you should be with your current love, ask this question rather than a lot of questions around the main problem.

Ask me, "what if I stay? What happens if I leave? Will I be happy if I stay? Will anything change if I stick to it?" These questions will give you the real answers you need to help you solve your problems with love and relationship.

Often a tarot reader can leave out important information that appears in the cards if you strictly focus on the question you asked when you have a lot. So, give the big picture at the beginning and all your questions so that you can get the best possible reading tarot love, and you will not be disappointed.

Love Tarot Reading and the Devil Tarot Card

Perhaps one of the scariest cards for reading love tarot is the devil's card. The image of the devil raises fear, uncertainty, and concern. However, in most love tarot figures, The Devil's Tarot card is often misunderstood. The Devil's Tarot should not be interpreted literally. In fact, this is a metaphor for our behavior and attachment to other people. In love tarot readings, the devil acts as a messenger. Its appearance guarantees reflection and a willingness to explore our behavior towards others.

The meaning of the tarot card of the devil's Tarot card traditionally refers to the issues of materialism and egocentrism. This is a warning that you can abuse their energy or influence. It also refers to self-pity, and the insatiable need to fulfill one's most primitive desires. The devil is a Tarot card that forces you to enter their shadow and realize their darkest impulses. In the end, you need to cope with these impulses and learn to control them. The devil reminds us that if we are not informed of our behavior, we are slaves to them.

When reading tarot love, the devil's tarot cards often refer to their own emotional dependence on their romantic relationship. Basically, the Devil's Tarot card is a card of interdependence. When you become completely dependent on their partner, they lose their personal freedom. This kind of freedom comes in the form of inner independence: a person does not need to be chained to another person in order to feel whole and satisfied. Reading the Tarot of love, the devil may suggest that there are attachments that can greatly depend on the neighbor. The devil remembers that they have their own inner power and the ability to take care of you, whether they are in a relationship or not.

Another hint of the tarot card of the devil in love is his reference to past painful relationships. In this case, it is usually an unhealthy connection or a negative projection in their current relationship. The devil's map reminds us that man has become a slave to his past. Their romantic relationship can be affected by old wounds that have not been treated emotionally. The devil asks you to explore the nature of your current relationship. Now is the time to wonder if your relationship is healthy. Are you in bondage? Are you repeating past behavior? Is your relationship motivated by the needs of early childhood that have never been sufficiently met? Do you decide to stay in an unhealthy relationship because you are trying to heal old wounds?

In love tarot readings, the devil's Tarot card pushes you to become conscious. It is a map that guarantees attention and reflection. The devil wants us to look inside and study our impulses and needs. Are we slaves to them? If so, how can we free ourselves? When it comes to romantic relationships, the devil reminds us that we have the power to choose the relationships we want. It reminds us that we must be ready to face our past fears and wounds, to find personal freedom and integrity.

Love Tarot Reading and the Justice Card

When the Justice Tarot card appears in a love tarot reading, you can be sure that the issues of balance and equity affect your relationship. The tarot card of justice often indicates that the relationship may require overwork. It is necessary to achieve mutual understanding and acceptance in order to advance the relationship. This is often achieved through compromise, donation, and reception. When you read love tarot cards, the tarot card pushes you to use your emotions and think objectively. It's time you told your partner the truth.

Justice often appears in a love tarot reading When relationship cycles are nearing completion. That is, the relationship is at a crossroads, where it can hesitate or move forward in a new direction. Justice tells us that this is a moment of reflection, where the strengths and weaknesses of relations must be subjected to close control. Both partners must be responsible and take responsibility for their behavior and actions. Justice tells us that it's time to be honest and put things in order so that the relationship can grow and prosper. Or, otherwise, the relationship could be in serious danger.

If you find yourself in a desperate situation with your partner, do not feel discouraged, because the Charter of justice often indicates great changes in the relationship, this may be true. However, you are not yet aware of it. This can be a good time to reach out to your partner to express your concerns. Communication and attentive listening can have a huge impact on your relationship. Sharing your feelings can certainly encourage sincerity, openness, and integrity. When this is achieved, conflicts will occur much less, and old anxieties and tensions can be replaced by a new understanding and a New Balance found.

The disadvantage is that the Inverted Tarot card Justice may indicate that you are forced to make uncomfortable decisions, which is struggling with divorce, divorced, or custody issues. When reading, tarot love can reverse the Charter of Justice refer to a one-sided relationship or lack of balance between partners. There may be legal problems, or the relationship may be full of hatred, lack of responsibility, or a partner, who may be treating others unfairly. The reverse Charter of justice can also serve as a warning that you or your partner is too strict or categorical. In such cases, it is important that both partners are honest, open, and willing to work to find a solution.

Do not be discouraged too much if you cannot. Be honest with yourself and continue your actions, even if the situation you are experiencing is difficult. In the end, the decision you make will always be right if you stay honest.

Love Tarot Reading and the Magician Card

In love tarot readings, the Magician represents the elements of spells and magic that is found in our relationships. It represents the creative power behind attraction, love, and Union. His appearance in love tarot reading often means a period of mania and magnetism. This presence should justify the excitement and caution because the mage has an irregular nature, and the energy around him can be intense and powerful.

Traditionally, the Tarot card is a manifestation card. His reminder is that his ideas can be consolidated into a particular reality. The magician is an action card and learned to direct the divine energy into the physical plane. In other words, The Magician creates with the help of the divine. It is a conscious connection between the deity and the kingdom of man. It is a map of creation that shows its forces in the everyday world.

In love reading tarot, the magic of a magician can bring together two people. If you were looking for a new partnership, it would be time to put your creative energy to use and confidence in the process. The magician makes you feel the strength in you and recognize that you have the power to create your own reality. Using your own self-confidence can help you make important connections. If you are already in a relationship, then "magic is in the air" It's time to explore with your partner. Your joint efforts could yield lasting results.

In reading the tarot of love, a magician can also represent a significant love or other interest. The magician can also point to an individual who has learned to control the world around him in order to achieve his goals. He is a person who wants to stay active and constantly tries to make things move. He is a man who knows how to use his abilities to create the world he wants. It can be a beautiful speaker and adaptable to any situation you are in.

A negative element of the magician of Tarot Cards is his vulnerability to cheating. In this regard, it can be false or lead to false intentions. When tarot figures appear in love, he always represents a person you need to know before you give him your heart.

Love tarot Reading and the Sun Card

In love tarot readings, The Sun Tarot card is the card of joy, happiness, and fulfillment. The solar card reminds you of confidence. This trust will be the light that shines in your relationship. Thanks to its appearance, you can be sure that your love relationships will reach a new level of connection and harmony. And most importantly, your intuition will lead you into your love relationships.

Tarot sun card traditionally represents success. The sun often brings news about weddings, births, financial results, celebrations, the completion of important projects, and joy. The sun represents a new perspective and clarity. A person achieved internal integrity when his unconscious and consciousness United.

As for the love life, The Sun is a positive sign. The sun indicates a period of celebration and happiness. If you are in a serious relationship, then this happiness will be shared between you and your partner. There will be new levels of mutual understanding and compassion. As for the love of Tarot data, the sun can refer to family affairs. In some cases, the sun may refer to pregnancy and/or the beginning of a new family.

For a man, the sun reminds you to get there. Now it's time to celebrate who you are. There's a good chance you'll meet someone new. If you have enjoyed one in the past, you may be ready to look for another significant one. In the love tarot, The Sun can mean a new relationship and often refers to the realization of desire.

Finally, The Sun Tarot card encourages you to become playful. Whether you're in a relationship or not, now is the time to enjoy life. Get ready to drain your inner Baby. The ultimate goal is to express yourself without self-awareness or fear. In love tarot readings, the sun serves as a reminder to always be your true self.

Traditional Tarot

The tradition of Tarot is estimated at more than five hundred years, with archetypal roots, which can be traced almost two thousand years. Traditional tarot gave way to modern methods of divination, but still remains a reservoir of ancient wisdom. Traditional tarot cards are the original source of modern playing cards.

The history and origin of the Tarot are not entirely clear. However, many theories support the belief about its origin from various places such as China, India, or Egypt. The oldest tarot cards that were found, however, dated back to the fifteenth century and were found in Spain, Italy, and France. According to historical evidence, traditionally, tarot cards were used as playing cards with pictures that showed living conditions, liberal arts, and virtues such as temperance and prudence. It is generally believed that, initially, tarot cards were not used as a means of divination.

Traditional tarot cards have been adapted to the current styles, and the Tarot Cards of the rider-Waite, the tarot card of Aquarius, the tarot card of Crowley Thoth, and the Tarot Card of Cagliostro are now considered to be the most basic and traditional tarot cards. These maps are designed based on historical maps and are considered an ideal option for beginners. Rider-Waite Tarot was designed in 1909 by artist Pamela Coleman Smith, according to specifications provided by Arthur Edward Waite. This pack contains seventy-eight cards with 56 smaller Arcane cards and 22 major mysterious cards. But the package has revolutionized traditional decks by assigning images to smaller mysterious cards. This deck is the most popular tarot deck in the world, which is preferred by beginners and advanced tarot students.

However, most tarot historians consider the entire tarot decks used in practice before the nineteenth century as historical bridges. Traditional tarot decks are considered strictly based on bridges, which prevailed at the time of Golden Dawn. Platinum A. E-mail. Waite and Pamela Coleman Smith are good examples of traditional tarot decks. These tarot decks further led to more popular board runners-Waite and deck Thoth.

Celtic Dragon Tarot

For the ancient Celts, the Dragon symbolized fertility or the creation of the Earth. They believed that a dragon formed the first cell born from the Earth and fertilized by the sky of wind and water. When the ancient Druids spoke of Celtic Dragons, they referred to dragon lines. These lines were considered places where most of the energetic, magical, and cosmic forces appeared on Earth and where their ritual meetings took place. They believed that dragons were creatures of a parallel world and, as such, sanctified these meeting places.

In mythology, King Arthur was overwhelmed by the dreams of dragons at the time of Mordred's conception and even before his own death. The Celts have long believed that when the King sces the Dragon, destruction will come to Earth. Still, it remains an important Celtic symbol depicted on the flag of Wales.

Tarot Dragon

Tarot cards of the Celtic Dragon have only been there for a few years. What makes it special, there are spells and meditations to accompany the bridge, which are intended to guide the reader through various exercises to invoke the energy of the Dragon and perform sacred visualization.

To illustrate this, each deck contains a spell for Prosperity. This means lighting a green and Golden candle. After they are placed on the altar with three specific cards, confirmation is repeated, and prosperity is welcomed.

Dragon tarot follows the same basic structure as traditional tarot cards. He has 78 cards, which are divided into four seeds are pentagrams, cups, swords, and wands. The cards correspond to wands with air and swords with fire. There are 22 major Arcane cards and 56 minor arcane cards.

The causes are represented as such.

Pentacles are given the sense of the Land Of Dragons involving elements of the earth, Northern energy, and physics

The cups have the meaning of water dragons and include elements of water, Western Energy and emotional

Swords stand behind fire dragons, and their corresponding elements are fire, south, and your energy.

Wands mean aerial Dragons with aerial, Oriental and mental elements

Small differences

There are some small changes in the names of the main Arcanes, and the names and numbers are displayed in Arabic numerals. Other changes are that The Hierophant will replace the High Priest, and chains will replace the devil. The formal ceremonial sectors of The Hierophant and the devil is not part of Celtic mythology these new representations of meaning.

Smaller bows use traditional outfits, but their corresponding elements are different. For example, wands are depicted as air instead of fire, and swords as fire instead of air.

The titles of the suit have not changed, and the cards of the court remain as king, queen, knight, and Page. It is worth noting that both sexes have changed; for example, a knight can be represented by a woman. Celtic does not discriminate against men and women, and it is common for men and women to work side by side. They went to war together, too. This aspect of Celtic tradition has been translated into these maps.

Changes in some photos are interesting and show that the magician is a woman. They also show that the High Priestess is active and dynamic. The women in these

Celtic Dragon Tarot Cards are portrayed as physically strong and powerful. Perhaps these representations are meant to mean what we know about the former Celtic Women.

Each card in the main Arcane has a full-size black and white image of each card and is accompanied by a keyword. Each card also receives a description, as well as a divine meaning, but there are no inverted meanings.

The creators of these Celtic tarot cards believe that the Dragon is dedicated to bringing radiant energy to life in the traditional tarot structure. Each image uses Dragons to reflect its meaning and uses backgrounds that reflect the Celtic history, culture, and symbols.

What makes this pack is excellent Celtic Dragon art on each card and on the back of each card is decorated with Celtic knot design.

A Tarot Spread and Unique Form of Tarot Reading

The Celtic spread of Tarot Cards is used for most of the data. It also refers to the unique form of Tarot and reading (but we'll talk about it later). Positions are numbers, and each number represents a specific context for each card.

They are as follows:

1. Current position (atmosphere in which the questioner is currently working)

2. Instantaneous influence (shows the nature of the influence or the obstacles that lie directly in front of it)

3. Purpose or Destiny (shows the purpose or destiny of the interviewer. It presents the best that can be achieved due to the existing circumstances)

4. Far into the past (shows great events and influences that existed in the past and are based on current events.)

5. Recent past events (shows recent events that affect the current location.)

6. Future influence (shows the sphere of influence that will come into being in the near future.)

7. Interviewer (shows the current location or interviewer's location. Try to put the question in the right point of view.)

8. Environmental factors (shows the influence of the interviewer on other people and events. It reveals trends and factors in relation to other people that can affect the partner.)

9. Inner emotions (they show the inner hopes and hidden emotions, desires, fears, and anxieties of the interviewer, including future thoughts.)

10. The final result (climax and results of all influences as revealed in the provided reading of the event and influences continue as stated.

Preservation of Celtic mythology

Few people realize that Celtic mythology is so fascinating and could be used on the side of the Tarot constructive path. Using the stories of Celtic mythology, we can gain greater depth and understanding of tarot reading. By interpreting these stories specifically, our unconscious minds allow them to become powerful tools to better understand our lives.

Celtic tarot cards were created as a way to restore the lost connection of Celtic mythology and Celtic art in the ancient wisdom of tarot cards. Combining the traditional meaning of tarot cards with popular characters from Celtic history, especially through the arturské tradition.

Celtic myth and legend, like tarot cards, come from a clear space and show us the portal that connects the spiritual world with our daily life. The typical art of Celtic Tarot, depicting the wonders of Celtic tradition and the wisdom of Tarot, combines to make this process a very pleasant experience.

Celtic Culture On The Brink Of Extinction

Its devoted followers strongly love pagan Celtic mythology. The world is probably very little of other cultures, which arouse as much interest as the Celtic people. However, over time, this culture has been obscured to the extent that it is suffocating and clear. The main contributors include Christianity, the Greek Zodiacs, and the Olympic Pantheon.

This unique version of the Tarot will be a great addition for those who practice the art of tarot, or for those who feel connected to the Celtic culture. Breast Art Maps is beautiful and provides a good way to help preserve Celtic history and tradition.

Tarot Symbolism and Meaning of the High Priestess Tarot Card

As for the symbolism of the Tarot, the card of the High Priestess is full of rich representative images and meanings. He is the embodiment of deep secrecy and secrecy. When she appears in the tarot reading, the High Priestess is a map of dreams, visions, and performances of all the secrets of the universe. It represents the intuitive female aspects of our media. As for development, he speaks of his inner voice and intuitive consciousness. It's an area of internal knowledge.

When reading the Tarot, the High Priestess is a female archetype. Unlike a magician who is active in nature, the High Priestess prefers passivity. It is associated with the unconscious, and its receptivity makes it an ideal female symbol. His receptive character allows him to explore the secrets and mysterious elements of the natural world.

The symbolism of Tarot number two: the tarot card of the High Priestess is the second card in the main Arcanes. Its connection with Number Two represents balance, harmony, and duality. In a tarot reading, the two often refer to the polarity, and if the card High

Priestess tarot number two refers to dualism found in the natural world and the psyche. The papacy represents a crossroads where two opposites meet. It has the ability to explore all Antipodes and use this energy to create something completely new.

The symbolism of the Tarot two pillars: in traditional tarot decks, the High Priestess is represented between two pillars, one black, and the other white. The pillars refer to the duality so often represented in the natural world: light and dark, night and day, birth and death, and positive and negative. Psychologically, both pillars relate to both male and female aspects of the psyche, as well as conscious and unconscious parts of the mind. Symbolically, this concerns her ability to plunge the High Priestess into the realm of the unconscious and carry her wisdom into conscious consciousness.

The symbolism of the tarot veil: behind the sitting priestess is a veil. The veil, a symbol of everything that remains invisible in the natural world, hides its hidden knowledge. The High Priestess serves as the guardian of secret wisdom. Its main purpose is to preserve everything that is considered sacred. When reading, the Tarot is a wise teacher and urges it to seek its own veil of rational thinking and look into their own unconscious wisdom.

The symbolism of the moon Tarot: in most tarot decks is the high priestess associated with the moon, which is usually represented by a crescent moon at his feet. The moon represents the female, emotional, unconscious, and intuitive elements of our psyche. It reminds us to rely on the soft light of the moon. This is the light of intuition. When reading the Tarot, the High Priestess presents our own inner knowledge. His connection with the Moon suggests that hidden knowledge can always be found in us.

The Moon also represents things that can remain invisible. The moon is a woman's night and often represents overshadowed aspects of the media. When reading the Tarot, the moon can be a symbol of the female mother, the inner child, and the influence of her subconscious.

The symbolism of the Tarot: on the knees of the priestess lies the role. In traditional tarot decks, the Scroll is associated with the Hebrew Torah. This concerns the need of the High Priestess to respect the Divine Laws of the natural world. It is also a scroll in which he records his memories. It represents all the knowledge and experience of the High Priestess. It serves as a container for mystery and mysterious knowledge, reflected in our world.

Discover the Meaning of the Chariot Tarot Card

The Chariot is the eighth card in the Order Of The Tarot game. Like the lover's card before, the Chariot also has a lot to do with the realm of emotions. However, it is important to note that the emotions involved are no longer in its pure and unlimited form. The car is about productivity and performance that occurs once you learn to control, channel, and tame your emotions and instincts. Only when you can control yourself Can you hope to control the world around you or any of the people in it.

The tank teaches us that the path to such mastery passes through the diligent self-discipline, which allows the use of a military symbol for the ideals that this card represents an incredibly appropriate. As well as the army promotes self-discipline and resilience through the difficult tactics so that new employees can better triumph under pressure, the car shows us the path to achievement and fulfillment through self-control and self-awareness. When we learn the lesson that you learn once and for all, we are not just a better survivor in the face of life's difficulties, but also more complete beings, ready for anything, what can life throw.

The traditional image of the tarot card of the tank depicts a royal male figure inside the tank itself. The vehicle itself is usually depicted as cartoons by two sphinxes of different colors, although there are many pictures of cars with traditional horses instead. Two sphinxes of different colors symbolize the opposite poles; positive and negative, dark and light, etc. The fact that the car driver successfully took advantage and used their innate power transfer from the place where they are, where they should be symbolizes the triumph of the human spirit over the challenge, adversity, instinct, and irrationality.

The image as a whole serves to remind us that while we are the people, we need our emotions, our driving force in the world, they are not productive forces, which may be if they are properly used and exploited. Instead of pain, anger, or other strong emotions and letting ourselves be consumed, we can channel them into productive activities that make us better.

When the Chariot appears in the spread of tarot cards, it usually means the presence of a situation where a similar control of emotions and instincts is needed.

The Quaker should not allow his energy to be wasted by self-pity, idleness, or fear. Instead, he should understand that he is asked to stand up, take control of himself for the better, and in the future, fight with the chin raised.

Kind reader,

Thank you very much. I hope you enjoyed the book.

Can I ask you a big favor?

I would be grateful if you would please take a few minutes to leave me a gold star on Amazon.

Thank you again for your support.

Rebecca Hood

Printed in Great Britain
by Amazon